Early Americas' Unsolved Mysteries

by Scott Gillam

Editorial Offices: Glenview, Illinois • Parsippany, New Jersey • New York, New York

Sales Offices: Needham, Massachusetts • Duluth, Georgia • Glenview, Illinois
Coppell, Texas • Sacramento, California • Mesa, Arizona

The Origins of the Early Americans

Where did our ancestors come from? What happened to them? Scientists who study these questions thought they had found the answer in the 1930s. During this period, scientists found unusual spear points near Clovis, New Mexico. Using the carbon 14 method of dating objects, or carbon dating, the scientists discovered that these spear points were about 13,500 years old. Similar spear points have been found at many other locations in North America.

Scientists had studied the changing climate of North America knew that during this same period the Bering Land Bridge between Asia and North America had existed. The land bridge had been formed when the sea level dropped dramatically during the last Ice Age. This geological change produced hundreds of thousands of square miles of new land between the two continents. Scientists also knew that humans who hunted large animals to survive were living in Siberia during this period. Scientists put together the evidence about early humans in Siberia, the similarity in the time of appearance of the spear points found in North America, and the presence of the land bridge. Scientists concluded that the earliest humans to enter North America were hunters from Siberia about fourteen thousand years ago who were pursuing wild game.

Clovis points were attached to spear handles using leather straps as fasteners.

Problems with the Clovis Theory of Origin

Some scientists disagree with the Clovis theory of a single point of human entry into North America fourteen thousand years ago. They note that the Native Americans of North America and South America were quite different from one another. They spoke different languages, looked different, and had different cultures. In addition, these scientists ask why early travelers to an uncrowded land like the Americas would have wanted to keep moving further south once they entered North America because they had no pack animals or wheels to help them. Finally, these scientists note that there is no direct evidence linking the Clovis people with prehistoric Siberian hunters. Some recent finds in North America appear to be older than Clovis. All these points raise serious doubts about the Clovis theory of a single time and place of original entry into North America.

The Earliest American Empire

The Olmec were the first people in the Americas to form an empire for which we have any evidence. More than 3,000 years ago they settled along the Gulf Coast of Mexico just west of the Yucatan **Peninsula**. Like all the early settled communities in the Americas, the Olmec were a farming culture. They used **aqueducts** to transport drinking water. Olmec farming efforts were successful enough to allow some people to become artists and builders instead of farmers. The artists created giant sculptures of heads from stone that was transported, probably by water, fifty miles to the capital at La Venta. They also created small figures of bald-headed babies. The Olmec built large platform mounds as temples to reflect their religious beliefs. Also, the Olmec used two kinds of calendars, one of which had 365 days.

The End of the Olmec

Did the Olmec migrate east toward Maya centers? Were they destroyed by violent internal conflicts? Half the monuments in one Olmec center were brutally destroyed, suggesting a violent clash.

The suddenness of the Olmec downfall has led some to believe that perhaps an epidemic disease was responsible for their disappearance. These are the questions that surround the mystery of how the Olmec came to their end.

This giant half human-half jaguar god dates from the earliest phase of Olmec civilization. The Olmec also used two different types of calendars and developed a form of writing.

5

The Beginning and End of the Maya

Like the Olmec before them and the later Aztec and Inca civilizations, the Maya civilization that arose around 2000 B.C. led to many cultural, scientific, and political achievements. The Maya calendar, astronomical records, and method of writing on bark paper were highly advanced. Mayan records were kept on a **codex**. Most collections of these codices were unfortunately destroyed by the Spanish and others. Mayan cities were governed independently of one another. These cities formed **alliances** with, or fought wars against, other Mayan cities. Many people think of Mexico when the word *Maya* is mentioned. However, in addition to large territories in present-day southern Mexico, the Mayan Empire extended into Guatemala, Belize, Honduras, and El Salvador as well.

Explanations for the end of the "golden age" of the Maya around A.D. 900 have included everything from extreme weather and epidemics to foreign invasion and social revolution. One current theory stresses the interaction of population growth and food shortages. The soil was being exhausted and the forests were cut down due to population demands for more food and farmland. Farm workers were forced to find work in the cities to satisfy the demands of the upper classes for servants, builders, and artists. It is even possible that as economic conditions got worse, the kings and nobles of the upper class were killed by the people who blamed them for their problems. The Maya, however, did not completely die out. In fact, there are some four million of them living today, mostly in Guatemala and Mexico.

This ceramic figure of a Maya ruler was made between A.D. 600 and A.D. 800, the height of Maya civilization. It stands about eleven inches high and shows the ruler in war dress.

The Rise and Fall of
the Aztec Warrior Society

The fall of the Maya roughly coincided with the rise of the Aztec in the Valley of Mexico around A.D. 1000. Said to have migrated from a place in northwestern Mexico known as Aztlán (ahz-TLAHN), the Aztecs built a great city called Tenochtitlán (te-noch-tee-TLAHN) in central Mexico beginning in A.D. 1325. According to Aztec myth, the war and sun god Huitzilopochtli (WEE-tsee-lo-poacht-lee) urged the Aztec to migrate. The Aztec expanded Tenochtitlán by adding **chinampas** connected by **causeways**. In contrast to the relatively slow growth of the Maya Empire, the Aztecs had created an empire of perhaps five million people in about two hundred years.

Every male Aztec was considered a warrior. Only those who had captured prisoners could advance through the ranks and wear feathers and leather bracelets. The two highest military ranks could wear jaguar skins and eagle helmets.

The Aztecs were a military society, but they were no match for Hernando Cortés, either in their strength or tactics. After landing in Mexico in 1519, the Spanish explorer was able to make alliances with traditional Aztec enemies and capture the Aztec leader, Moctezuma. Cortés eventually laid siege to Tenochtitlán and starved the Aztecs into surrendering. Within two years of his arrival, Cortés had conquered the Aztecs and had taken over much of present-day Mexico. It is estimated that in the century following the Spanish conquest, three quarters of the Native American population in Spain's territories in the Americas perished from violence or disease, such as smallpox and measles.

The Moche Civilization of Peru

Nine hundred years before the Aztec spread across Mexico, the Moche (MOH-cheh) people along the coastal area of Peru were uniting to become the earliest empire in the Americas. Perhaps originating in Central America, the Moche grew over the next several hundred years to a population of at least 100,000 living in an area the size of Vermont. The Moche people farmed and fished to survive, irrigating their fields extensively with water from nearby rivers and fishing in the Pacific Ocean's coastal waters. They grew enough food to trade with their neighbors and also indulged their artistic talents, mostly in elaborate ceramic design.

The Moche lived in a coastal desert area. As a result, they experienced periods of drought followed by heavy rain. One drought apparently lasted for nearly thirty years. The rains were caused by El Niño, a weather pattern that regularly brings warm water to Peru's coast. This pattern causes heavy rainfall, which causes flooding. These floods probably washed away much of the topsoil on which Moche farms depended. At the same time, strong offshore winds would have blown sand from the coastal beaches over the fields. These events made it even more difficult to grow crops and forced the Moche to move north along the coast. El Niño events also do great harm to any people who rely heavily on fishing coastal waters because the water gets considerably warmer and fish die. These are undoubtedly some of the reasons why the Moche had disappeared by about A.D. 800.

Moche pots showed the social level or occupation of the person, shown here by the type of clothing and the decorations. Warriors, for example, were often shown with clubs and shields.

CONQVISTA ESTA ENLA
ATAGVALPAINGACIVDA
E CAXAMARCA ENSVT RONOVSI

The Fate of the Inca Empire

Between A.D. 1100 and 1200 the Inca Empire began at the Peruvian city of Cusco, about 200 miles northwest of Lake Titicaca. Over the next three hundred years, the Inca Empire grew to occupy a land area equal to the size of Western Europe. Incan history and beliefs were probably recorded as illustrations in their finely woven tapestries and textiles, which unfortunately did not survive. The Inca did not write. We do know something about their civilization, however, from the information recorded on **quipus** (KEE-pooz).

In 1532 Francisco Pizarro (fran-SEES-koh pee-SAHR-roh) of Spain and his small army defeated the Inca with the help of smallpox and other diseases brought by the Spanish. An estimated two-thirds of the Inca people were killed in the fifty years after the Spanish arrived. A civil war followed the death of an Incan king by smallpox. Pizarro arrived during this conflict and seized the opportunity to try to turn the Inca against their new king, Atahualpa (ahtah-WAL-pah). Ultimately, Pizarro (who himself only had a small army) was able to deceive and capture Atahualpa and defeat the Inca without a major battle. Pizarro's only remaining problem was to exercise his control over the vast Inca Empire. He tried to repress Incan culture. However, thirteen million Andean people today still speak Quechua (KEHCH-wuh), the ancient language of the Inca.

In this painting the captured Incan leader Atahualpa promises to fill a room with gold in return for his life. The gold was collected, but Pizarro, reacting to a rumor that a rebellion would try to free the Incan king, had Atahualpa executed anyway.

What happened to the Anasazi?

Remains of **pit houses** and **pueblos**, the latter made of sandstone or **adobe**, are evidence of an ancient culture that began in the southwestern United States about A.D. 100. The first Anasazi may have come from the Mogollon (moh-GOH-yohn) people who lived in the same general area. Anasazi communities, though small and isolated, were connected by trade routes and at their peak inhabited an area the size of South Carolina.

Scientists propose several theories about why the Anasazi suddenly abandoned their pueblos in the late 1200s. Prolonged drought by itself or in combination with dramatic climate change may have left the Anasazi unable to grow food. Population increase may have led to social unrest. There is also the possibility that the Anasazi suffered a religious crisis since their old religious symbols are not found in the new places they moved. More than one of these theories of why the Anasazi disappeared may be true.

Solving the Mystery of Early Americans' Origins

We have seen how different the various groups who first inhabited the Americas were, along with the different places they are said to have come from. The Aztec, among others, were notably warlike and brutal while the Anasazi were mostly peaceful. The Aztec and Maya are thought to have come from Mexico, while the Anasazi originated in the southwestern United States. The Moche, forerunners of the Inca, probably began in Peru.

As scientists continue to look for evidence of early humans in the Americas, their recent discoveries may support the theory that these first settlers originally came from different places. The remains of the 9,000-year-old Kennewick Man have been found near the Columbia River in Washington State. Scientists today are still unsure about who Kennewick Man was and what his origins are.

As scientists' tools for determining the age and characteristics of early humans continue to become more accurate, it seems likely that even more startling discoveries lie ahead. Given this fact, it would seem reasonable to keep an open mind about the origins of the early Americans.

The original Anasazi left suddenly, but their descendants still live in the same area of the United States. These Pueblo in Acoma, for example, live in one of the oldest continuously inhabited communities in the United States. Pueblo have been living there since the 1100s.

Glossary

adobe building material made of mud and straw that is dried in the sun

alliance an agreement made between two or more groups or nations

aqueduct a structure used to carry flowing water from a distance

causeway a raised bridge made of land

chinampa a man-made island

codex a folding-screen book containing information about predicting the future and religious rituals

peninsula land that is nearly surrounded by water

pit house a house made from digging a hole in the ground and covering it with logs

pueblo a structure of adobe brick

quipu a knotted rope used by the Inca to keep records